Date:

MW01243184

Moms name:

Dads name:

Whats the story of "figuring out the pregnancy?

Baby

Which gender?

Moms guess:

Dads guess:

Height at birth?

Moms guess:

Dads guess:

Weight at birth?

Moms guess:

Dads guess:

Date:

Pregnancy is going to alter your thinking forever, it's going to make you realize how fragile and important life is and why it must be protected at all cost.

Which values shall the grow up with?

Moms values:

Dads values:

Baby values:

Is this your first child?

Mom:

Dad:

Shall the child have a religious upbringing?

Mom:

Dad:

Final decision:

Name?

Girl:

Boy:

Date:

Shall the child follow your national child vaccination program?

Mom:

Dad:

Final decision:

Shall the birth be at a private clinic or a hospital?

Mom:

Dad:

Final decision:

Where shall the first Christmas as parents be?

Our Place ☐ Granny's ☐ Uncle's ☐ Other ☐

Others?:

What defines a good parent?

Mom:

Dad:

Date:

What kind of skills does the mother you want to be have?

What kind of skills does the father you want to be have?

Do you have any bad habits you need to eliminate before birth?

Mom:

Dad:

2022

Set a ring around the presumed day of birth

January

Mo	Tu	We	Th	Fr	Sa	Su
					1	2
3	4	5	6	7	8	9
10	11	12	13	14	15	16
17	18	19	20	21	22	23
24	25	26	27	28	29	30
31						

February

Mo	Tu	We	Th	Fr	Sa	Su
	1	2	3	4	5	6
7	8	9	10	11	12	13
14	15	16	17	18	19	20
21	22	23	24	25	26	27
28						

March

Mo	Tu	We	Th	Fr	Sa	Su
	1	2	3	4	5	6
7	8	9	10	11	12	13
14	15	16	17	18	19	20
21	22	23	24	25	26	27
28	29	30	31			

April

Mo	Tu	We	Th	Fr	Sa	Su
				1	2	3
4	5	6	7	8	9	10
11	12	13	14	15	16	17
18	19	20	21	22	23	24
25	26	27	28	29	30	

May

Mo	Tu	We	Th	Fr	Sa	Su
						1
2	3	4	5	6	7	8
9	10	11	12	13	14	15
16	17	18	19	20	21	22
23	24	25	26	27	28	29
30	31					

June

Mo	Tu	We	Th	Fr	Sa	Su
		1	2	3	4	5
6	7	8	9	10	11	12
13	14	15	16	17	18	19
20	21	22	23	24	25	26
27	28	29	30			

July

Mo	Tu	We	Th	Fr	Sa	Su
				1	2	3
4	5	6	7	8	9	10
11	12	13	14	15	16	17
18	19	20	21	22	23	24
25	26	27	28	29	30	31

August

Mo	Tu	We	Th	Fr	Sa	Su
1	2	3	4	5	6	7
8	9	10	11	12	13	14
15	16	17	18	19	20	21
22	23	24	25	26	27	28
29	30	31				

September

Mo	Tu	We	Th	Fr	Sa	Su
			1	2	3	4
5	6	7	8	9	10	11
12	13	14	15	16	17	18
19	20	21	22	23	24	25
26	27	28	29	30		

October

Mo	Tu	We	Th	Fr	Sa	Su
					1	2
3	4	5	6	7	8	9
10	11	12	13	14	15	16
17	18	19	20	21	22	23
24	25	26	27	28	29	30
31						

November

Mo	Tu	We	Th	Fr	Sa	Su
	1	2	3	4	5	6
7	8	9	10	11	12	13
14	15	16	17	18	19	20
21	22	23	24	25	26	27
28	29	30				

December

Mo	Tu	We	Th	Fr	Sa	Su
			1	2	3	4
5	6	7	8	9	10	11
12	13	14	15	16	17	18
19	20	21	22	23	24	25
26	27	28	29	30	31	

Date:

Mamas best story of daddy, for your child to read some day

Date:

Daddy's best story of mama, for your child to read some day

Date:

Mother, which of daddy's traits, do you hope the child will get?

Daddy, which of mama's traits, do you hope the child will inherit?

Whom shall be the Godfather/Mother?

Mom:

Dad:

Final decision:

First one you want to tell about the pregnancy?

Mom:

Dad:

How do you want to tell it?

Mom:

Dad:

Date:

How did people react?

Journal

Journal your thoughts, talks and ideas

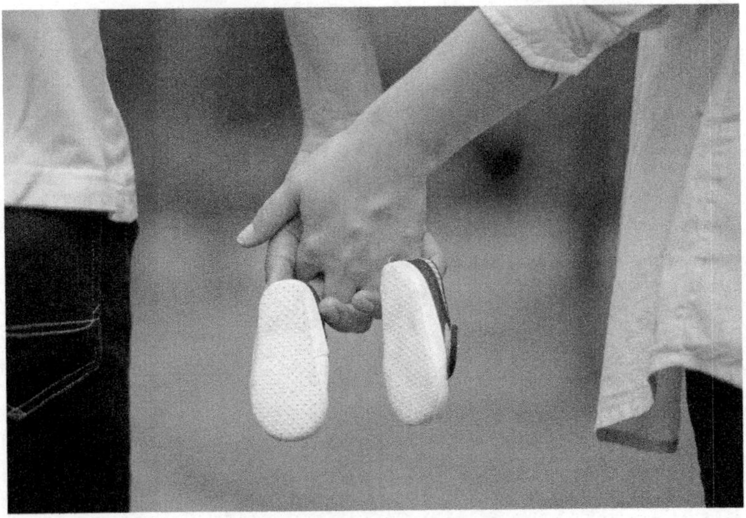

Here are some ideas:

- Write a pregnancy journal for you child to read someday
- Stories of both of your parents
- What is/was good about them?
- Write a poem
- Write a letter to your child
- What are grateful for?
- How did you guys meet?

Feel free to glue photos inside the journal

Date:

Date:

Date:

Date:

Date:

Date:

Date:

Date:

Date:

Date:

Date:

Date:

Date:

Date:

Date:

Date:

Date:

Date:

Date:

Date:

Date:

Date:

Date:

Date:

Date:

Date:

Date:

Date:

Date:

Date:

Date:

Date:

Date:

Date:

Date:

Date:

Date:

Date:

Date:

Date:

Date:

Date:

Date:

Date:

Date:

Date:

Date:

Date:

Date:

Date:

Date:

Date:

Date:

Date:

Date:

Date:

Date:

Date:

Date:

Date:

Date:

Date:

Date:

Date:

Date:

Date:

Date:

Date:

Date:

Date:

Date:

Date:

Date:

Date:

Date:

Date:

Date:

Date:

Date:

Thank you!

Keep this journal a save place for your kids to read one day

Find more useable tools at MortenCharlie.com

Made in the USA
Middletown, DE
15 February 2022

61222220R00056